My Christian Passport

belongs to

Name

Address

Telephone

Put
a recent photo
of yourself
here.

My Family
me
father
mother
paternal grandmother
maternal grandmother
paternal grandfather
maternal grandfather

Birth

Date

Place

City or town

Country

“You are my...Beloved;
my favour rests on you.”
(Mark 1:11)

"I have called you
by your name."
(Isaiah 43:1)

Baptism

Celebrated on the ___ day of_______, _______, at

Church

Street

City or town

Country

Diocese

Sponsors/

Godparents

Priest or deacon

Baptismal names

Meaning of my first name

The priest or deacon can sign
his name or put the parish seal here.

"I bless you, Father, Lord of Heaven and of earth, for hiding these things from the learned and clever and revealing them to mere children."
(Matthew 11:25)

"I call you friends because I have made known to you everything I have learned from my Father."
(John 15:15)

My Religious Education

(Here are some of the programs, teachers, years, special moments)

First Reconciliation

Celebrated on the ____ day of ________, _____, at

Church

City and country

Catechist

Priest

“Father, I have sinned against heaven and before you.”
(Luke 15:18)

First Communion

Celebrated on the ____ day of ________, _____, at

Church

City and country

Catechist

Priest

"Do this
in memory of me."
(Luke 22:19)

"Each one of you has received a special grace, so, like good stewards responsible for all these different graces of God, put yourselves at the service of others."
(1 Peter 4:10)

Christian Activities

in your family, your parish, your school, Christian groups and clubs

"Did not our hearts burn within us as he talked to us on the road and explained the scriptures to us?"
(Luke 24:32)

"What the Spirit brings is very different: love, joy, peace, patience, kindness, goodness, trustfulness, gentleness and self-control."
(Galatians 5:22)

Confirmation

Celebrated on the ____ day of ________, _____, at

Church

City and country

Diocese

Confirmed by

(name of bishop or his delegate)

Prepared by

(name of catechist or teacher)

Sponsor

The bishop or his delegate can sign his name or put the parish seal here.

Prayer to Discern My Calling

Loving Creator,
You call me by name,
as you call all Christians,
asking me to
make known your love.

To help complete Jesus' work,
you make us his disciples.
Help us to spread the Gospel,
to make known your name
to all the nations.

Protect us, the children of the world,
and send us your Spirit.
Grant us speed and generosity
in answering your call,
and give us the strength to follow you,
for you are love.
Amen.

Called to Serve

Jesus invites me to explore the many ways in which I can serve others in the Church: as a committed lay person, as a priest, as a missionary, as a deacon, as a religious brother or sister.

A Note to Parents and Catechists

How to Use My Christian Passport

You can present this booklet to the child at any time during the sacramental initiation process, regardless of the child's age. It will be a companion throughout the different stages of Christian initiation.

If the booklet is given to the parents at the time of the child's baptism, it can be symbolically presented to the child during the baptism ceremony as a sign of the new responsibilities that are involved in the journey of faith now being undertaken.

To make *My Christian Passport* "official," you can have the priest or pastoral worker sign it or affix the seal of the parish.

Design, illustrations and layout: Anna Payne-Krzyzanowski

1 Eglinton Avenue East, Suite 800, Toronto, ON M4P 3A1
www.novalis.ca
ISBN 13: 978-2-89507-151-8

Published in the United States by The Liturgical Press.
ISBN 13: 978-0-8146-1576-8

Printed in China • Reprint 2021